WASHINGTON AND TWO MARCHES 1963 & 1983

THE THIRD AMERICAN REVOLUTION

by
Frederick Walton Yette
and
Samuel F. Yette

Designed by
James A. Davis Advertising and Design
Art Direction, Bruce Fagin
Michael Lewis Yette, Consultant

COTTAGE BOOKS
P.O. Box 2071
Silver Spring, Md. 20902

ISBN 0-911253-02-5 (Cloth-bound)
ISBN 0-911253-03-3 (Paper-bound)

Copyright ©1984 by
Frederick Walton Yette and Samuel F. Yette

Library of Congress Catalog Card Number: 83-073338
PRINTED IN THE UNITED STATES OF AMERICA

PERMISSIONS

For permission to quote from or copy copyrighted or otherwise special works, the authors are grateful to the following:

Joan Daves, for permission to quote from "I Have a Dream," a speech by Dr. Martin Luther King, Jr., at the Lincoln Memorial, August 28, 1963.

Charles Jacobs, of Galerie Triangle, Washington, D.C., for permission to copy his calligraph of "I Have a Dream," by Dr. Martin Luther King, Jr.

Robert D. Lutz, editor of *Photographer's Market,* 1984 Edition, for permission to excerpt a "Close-up" biographical feature on Samuel F. Yette, photojournalist.

Typography by Robey Graphics

Printed by Colortone
Washington, D.C.

To Our Dear Wife and Mother

Sadie Walton Yette
(1934-1983)

Whose gentle, loving strength, courage, and wisdom symbolized the enduring qualities of Black women in America, who, in the face of over-whelming odds, made some positive change—the Third American Revolution—not only possible, but also inevitable.
With eternal love and dedication.

Contents

Introduction

This is a book about the Third American Revolution and its two major marches. It is also about how men, women, and children of cosmic courage and genius have used the First Amendment as a major revolutionary weapon.

The First American Revolution, of course, ended with British General Charles Cornwallis' surrender to General George Washington at Yorktown, Va., in 1781.

The Second American Revolution, the Civil War, legally freed the nation from its own racial enslavement. It ended with Confederate General Robert E. Lee's surrender to General Ulysses S. Grant at Appomattox, Va., in 1865.

Each of the first two revolutions ended years of bloody struggle and the loss of many thousands of lives—on both sides.

The Third American Revolution has not ended. But it has begun. It has been a struggle of generations, and, like the others, this one has taken and broken many lives. But, unlike the others, victims in the Third American Revolution have been almost entirely on one side—those already suffering injustice and seeking relief.

Also unlike the others, the heroes in this war are an army of non-violent combatants.

It is essentially a war in which the majorities have for centuries deprived minorities, mainly "Indians" and Afro-Americans, of life, liberty and property, or—in a word—justice, in economic, social, and survival terms.

The newest revolution, by masses alternately calling themselves "A Coalition of Conscience" and "The Rainbow Coalition," seeks to end the privations—including war itself—and to establish justice.

Because the new revolutionaries do not seek victory *over* anyone, theirs is a distinctly different kind of war. By those aggrieved, at least, it is a peaceful, healing war. It is a fight for power and change—but through persuasion—to achieve justice.

The social and political fabric of U.S. society is woven from two rather fragile strands. They hold that

(1) If ideas, ideologies, and information freely abound; that if truth and falsehood are permitted to grapple—fight it out—the people will know what is right and true; and that

(2) If they know right from wrong, the people will, at least gradually, choose to do right.

These are the daily tests of the First Amendment, and, indeed, the test of democratic rule.

The enduring genius of the democratic form is what the Frenchman, Alexis de Tocqueville, called "the sovereignty of the people" over any person, class, or government. In *Democracy in America,* de Tocqueville wrote:

If there is one country in the world where one can hope to appreciate the true value of the dogma of the sovereignty of the people, study its application to the business of society, and judge both its dangers and its advantages, that country is America.

As the victim of any lynching would attest, the danger of majority rule is that mere numerical superiority does not guarantee justice. The justice must derive, at best, from due process of laws based in reason and morality.

The "true value" of popular sovereignty, however, is a minority's ability to appeal to and persuade the majority to the side of justice, or at least to a favorable point of view amongst competing interests.

Ultimately, given that ability to inform and persuade, a minority view can attain majority status, and its proponents parity and power. It is this appeal and persuasive power that is the thrust of this ongoing Third American Revolution.

With that thrust, the late Dr. Martin Luther King, Jr., the greatest orator and spiritual leader in the nation's history, became a successful "drum major for justice," the appellation he modestly chose for himself.

Dr. King, with his magnificent "I Have a Dream" speech, electrified the nation as he led more than 250,000 on a "March on Washington for Jobs and Freedom," in 1963.

The Third American Revolution has known many marches. Some, like the 1965 march from Selma to Montgomery, were bloody and inhumane. But the most splendid and powerful of the marches have been the 1963 march, and "The 20th Anniversary March for Jobs, Peace, and Freedom" in 1983.

That they were powerful, in the best use of the First Amendment, is a matter of public record and consequence.

The 1963 march brought unprecedented civil rights gains, established the rightness of the revolution in the mind of the nation, and taught two generations—regardless of their causes—how to stand up and be counted.

The memory of Dr. King widens and continues this Third American Revolution. Indeed, it was his spirit that permeated the march of some half-million in 1983.

At the time of the 1963 march, there were only a few dozen Black mayors in the United States. At the time of the 1983 march, however, 244 U.S. cities had Black mayors.

The cities themselves—their sizes and locations—are as significant as the phenomenal increase in the number of cities having elected Black mayors. The cities included Atlanta, Birmingham, Chicago, Detroit, Gary, Los Angeles, New Orleans, Richmond, Tuskegee, and Washington, D.C., the nation's capital. Within two months after the August 27,

"Congress shall make no law respecting an establishment of religion, or prohibiting the free exercise thereof; or abridging the freedom of speech or of the press; or the right of the people peaceably to assemble, and to petition the government for a redress of grievances."

—The First Amendment, Constitution of the United States

1983 march, Philadelphia had been added to the list of cities with Black mayors.

In many of those cities, racial rebellions and police riots reigned during the 1960s and 1970s. It did not win the war, but the 1983 march did signal a new beginning. It formed an unprecedented coalition of petitioners, institutionalized the rightness of the revolution by winning a national holiday observance for Dr. King's birthday, and it arguably launched its own presidential candidate—the Rev. Jesse Jackson.

Further, while there were only four Black members of Congress at the time of the 1963 march, an unprecedented 21 Black members were seated in Congress at the time of the 1983 march.

Significantly also, in 1983, Guion Bluford, a Black U.S. astronaut, took his place in space, and Vanessa Williams, a 20-year-old talented New Yorker, became the first Black woman chosen "Miss America."

And yet, the millenium—victory in the form of a surrender by greedy and oppressive forces—is far in the distance.

Particularly in their poverty, and in their fight against technological displacement and social control, ordinary people continue a literal struggle for survival.

Two months after the 1983 march, hearings in Congress indicated that the nation's poor were getting poorer. They fell from a poverty gap of $28.9 billion in 1967 to a gap of $45.3 billion in 1983. That is the gap between the actual incomes of the poor and the official federal non-poor income levels.

These two factors—(1) increasing threats to the survival of huddled masses, and (2) inspired successful challenges for political power by their leaders—stress both the need for and the hope of such challenges.

Thus, the enormously dramatic marches of 1963 and 1983 have been two singularly successful catalytic events in a socio-political revolution. It is a Third American Revolution, a struggle whose consequences cannot with certainty be foretold, but whose presence, in 1983, became undeniable.

FOUR SCORE AND SEVEN YEARS AGO OUR FATHERS BROUGHT FORTH ON THIS CONTINENT A NEW NATION CONCEIVED IN LIBERTY AND DEDICATED TO THE PROPOSITION THAT ALL MEN ARE CREATED EQUAL ·
NOW WE ARE ENGAGED IN A GREAT CIVIL WAR TESTING WHETHER THAT NATION OR ANY NATION SO CONCEIVED AND SO DEDICATED CAN LONG ENDURE · WE ARE MET ON A GREAT BATTLEFIELD OF THAT WAR · WE HAVE COME TO DEDICATE A PORTION OF THAT FIELD AS A FINAL RESTING PLACE FOR THOSE WHO HERE GAVE THEIR LIVES THAT THAT NATION MIGHT LIVE · IT IS ALTOGETHER FITTING AND PROPER THAT WE SHOULD DO THIS · BUT IN A LARGER SENSE WE CAN NOT DEDICATE ~ WE CAN NOT CONSECRATE ~ WE CAN NOT HALLOW ~ THIS GROUND · THE BRAVE MEN LIVING AND DEAD WHO STRUGGLED HERE HAVE CONSECRATED IT FAR ABOVE OUR POOR POWER TO ADD OR DETRACT · THE WORLD WILL LITTLE NOTE NOR LONG REMEMBER WHAT WE SAY HERE BUT IT CAN NEVER FORGET WHAT THEY DID HERE · IT IS FOR US THE LIVING RATHER TO BE DEDICATED HERE TO THE UNFINISHED WORK WHICH THEY WHO FOUGHT HERE HAVE THUS FAR SO NOBLY ADVANCED · IT IS RATHER FOR US TO BE HERE DEDICATED TO THE GREAT TASK REMAINING BEFORE US ~ THAT FROM THESE HONORED DEAD WE TAKE INCREASED DEVOTION TO THAT CAUSE FOR WHICH THEY GAVE THE LAST FULL MEASURE OF DEVOTION ~ THAT WE HERE HIGHLY RESOLVE THAT THESE DEAD SHALL NOT HAVE DIED· IN VAIN ~ THAT THIS NATION UNDER GOD SHALL HAVE A NEW BIRTH OF FREEDOM ~ AND THAT GOVERNMENT OF THE PEOPLE BY THE PEOPLE FOR THE PEOPLE SHALL NOT PERISH FROM THE EARTH ·

U.S. Capitol dome

"All legislative powers herein granted shall be vested in a Congress of the United States, which shall consist of a Senate and House of Representatives."
—Article I, Constitution of the United States

Interior of Capitol dome, Constantino Brumidi's fresco is allegory of original 13 colonies.

White House

The Supreme Court Building

"The executive power shall be vested in a President of the United States of America."
—Article II, Constitution of the United States

"The judicial power of the United States shall be vested in one Supreme Court, and in such inferior courts as the Congress may from time to time ordain and establish."
—Article III, Constitution of the United States

". . . to secure these rights, governments are instituted among men, deriving their just powers from the consent of the governed. . . ."

Washington: Symbol of Democracy

Now, as originally, the people of the world come to America.

Originally, some came in make-shift boats. They still do. But now some come in gigantic ocean-liners and in jumbo-jets; and some on foot, under barbed wire and radar sweeps. Some come just to see, to marvel perhaps at what the idea of democracy has wrought. Especially those who arrive via the escape routes hope to stay.

Even those who do not come in via the Atlantic, even if they have never read the beckoning, encouraging words on the Statute of Liberty, the multitudes still have a sense of the message: "Give me your tired, your poor, your huddled masses yearning to breathe free. . . ."

Originally, some others came to America under the force and inhumane degradation of slave ships; and now—ironically, or perhaps, quite logically—with more vigor and devotion than any others, their heirs strive to make America *be* America.

Like many others, Black Americans find the city of Washington a kind of mecca. Visitors come daily, hourly, even by the minute. Indeed, yearly, visitors come to Washington by the millions—4.6 million in 1982.

Why is coming to Washington so special?

Coming to Washington is special because Washington symbolizes what is special about America.

Though she is one of the most beautiful cities in the world, Washington's sheer physicality cannot and does not explain her.

Though she is the seat of national government and power, that also falls short of explanation.

And yet, her physicality and levers of power do attach to her true meaning, especially in three constitutionally symbolic edifices—the Capitol, the White House, and the Supreme Court Building—and in the three best-known national monuments.

The city's tallest edifice is the Washington Monument—555 feet high—in honor of the nation's first president. In his farewell address, George Washington counseled the nation:

The nation which indulges toward another an habitual hatred or an habitual fondness is in some degree a slave. It is a slave to its animosity or to its affection, either of which is sufficient to lead it astray from its duty and its interest.

The Jefferson Memorial honors the third president, Thomas Jefferson, who gave this nation the world's most famous and enviable Declaration of Independence. One sentence alone would justify honor to Jefferson: "We hold these truths to be self-evident; that all men are created equal; that they are endowed by their creator with certain unalienable rights; that among these are life, liberty, and the pursuit of happiness. . . ."

When the Daughters of the American Revolution refused to allow the great Black contralto, Marian Anderson, to sing at Constitution Hall in 1939, she sang anyway—before some 35,000, in front of the Lincoln Memorial, on Easter Sunday.

It is often to the Lincoln Memorial that people go when they need a special welcome, when they feel that the government needs reminding that it belongs to the people, and has a special mission to guarantee justice.

Abraham Lincoln, of course, was the Great Emancipator, for it was he who signed the Emancipation Proclamation to end slavery. But he was also the nation's Great Healer. His most famous words are the lines he scribbled on a piece of paper and delivered at the Gettysburg Cemetery in the midst of the Civil War: ". . . we here highly resolve . . . that this nation, under God, shall have a new birth of freedom; and that government of the people, by the people, for the people, shall not perish from the earth."

The people come to Washington because of its symbols—its historic promise. It's the people's city, and their own histories of overcoming give them pride and hope.

◀*Ronald Reagan's Presidential Inaugural, 1981*

Presidential power and prerogatives, while limited, are broad. In top photograph, President Jimmy Carter, in Rose Garden ceremony, welcomes Vice Premier Deng Hsaio Ping of Peoples' Republic of China, ending, in 1979, 30 years of isolation. White House visitor Billy Carter, brother of the President, holds court on the White House south lawn. Federal Bureau of Investigation (FBI) is symbolic of police powers of each President. Executive Office Building is nerve center of federal bureaucracy that includes staff of thousands. The President formulates foreign policy and is military Commander-in-Chief.

Basic rights are preserved in the Bill of Rights—the first 10 Amendments. First Amendment rights include freedom of religion, a vibrant part of life in Washington area: Worshippers at New Bethel Baptist Church. Mormon Tabernacle in Kensington, Md. Annual Pageant of Peace, on the mall south of the White House. Jewish Festival of Lights, in Lafayette Park, across from the White House. National Catholic Shrine. Washington's Episcopal Church of St. Peter and St. Paul, also known as the Washington National Cathedral, is burial site of World War I President Woodrow Wilson.

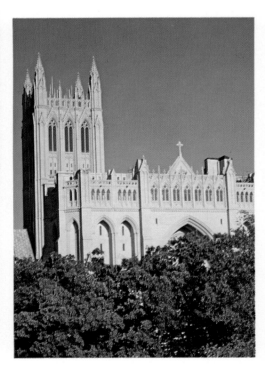

Freedom of Speech

Famous photographer P. H. Polk, of Tuskegee, Ala., tells of half-century of photography in the Old South, after opening exhibition of his works at prestigious Corcoran Gallery of Art, mecca for many famous and controversial artists.

"Were it left to me to decide whether we should have a government without newspapers, or newspapers, without a government, I should not hesitate a moment to prefer the latter (newspapers.)"

—Thomas Jefferson

Toiling in the night, journalists at The Washington Post produce one of the nation's most powerful news media; pursuit of the Watergate crimes and publication of the Pentagon Papers, among the paper's high marks. Closing of The Washington Star in 1981 left the world's number one news city with only one daily paper for a brief period. Library of Congress, one of the world's largest, serves the public as well as the Congress.

. . . And of the Press

Thousands assembled in Washington Convention Center to observe presidential bid announcement by the Rev. Jesse Jackson. Lunch time is occasion for government and other workers to assemble informally in Farragut Square Park. Government workers also share right of formal association and right to petition through their union, the American Federation of Government Employees.

Assembly and Petition

2 1963: They Had a Dream

I Have A Dream

I say to you today, my friends, that in spite of the difficulties and frustrations of the moment, I still have a dream. It is a dream deeply rooted in the American dream. I have a dream that one day this nation will rise up and live out the true meaning of its creed: "We hold these truths to be self-evident: that all men are created equal." I have a dream that one day on the red hills of Georgia the sons of former slaves and the sons of former slaveowners will be able to sit down together at the table of brotherhood. I have a dream that one day even the state of Mississippi, a desert state sweltering with the heat of injustice and oppression, will be transformed into an oasis of freedom and justice. I have a dream that my four little children will one day live in a nation where they will not be judged by the color of their skin but the content of their character. I have a dream today. I have a dream that one day the state of Alabama, whose governor's lips are presently dripping with the words of interposition and nullification, will be transformed into a situation where little black boys and girls will be able to join hands with little white boys and white girls and walk together as sisters and brothers. I have a dream today. I have a dream that one day every valley shall be exalted, every hill and mountain shall be made low, the rough places will be made plains, and the crooked places will be made straight, and the glory of the Lord shall be reveald, and all flesh shall see it together. This is our hope. This is the faith with which I return to the South. With this faith we will be able to hew out of the mountains of despair a stone of hope. With this faith we will be able to transform the jangling discords of our nation into a beautiful symphony of brotherhood. With this faith we will be able to work together, to pray together, to struggle together, to go to jail together, to stand up for freedom together, knowing that we will be free one day. This will be the day when all of God's children will be able to sing with new meaning "My country 'tis of thee, sweet land of liberty, of thee I sing. Land where my fathers died, land of the Pilgrim's pride, from every mountainside, let freedom ring." And if America is to be a great nation this must become true. So let freedom ring from the prodigies hilltops of New Hampshire. Let freedom ring from the mighty mountains of New York. Let freedom ring from the heightening Alleghenies of Pennsylvania. Let freedom ring from the snow-capped Rockies of Colorado. Let freedom ring from the curvaceous peaks of California. But not only that; Let freedom ring from Stone Mountain of Georgia. Let freedom ring from every hill and mole hill of Mississippi. From every mountainside, let freedom ring. When we let freedom ring, when we let it ring from every village and every hamlet, from every state and every city, we will be able to speed up that day when all of God's children, black men and white men, Jews and Gentiles, Protestants and Catholics, will be able to join hands and sing in the word of that old Negro spiritual, "Free at last! Free at last! Thank God almighty, we are free at last!"

Rev. Dr. Martin Luther King Jr.

January 15, 1929 - April 4, 1968

C. H. Jacobs Calligrapher

“Dreamers”: These hundreds of thousands of peaceful marchers joined Dr. Martin Luther King, Jr., in his historic and eloquent statement of his dream of a free and just nation. Often, out of respect, instead of applauding Dr. King's speech, the crowd just waved passionately.

DEDICATED TO THE PROPOSITION: Leaders of the 1963 March for "Jobs and Freedom" bowed in prayer during invocation by the Reverend Patrick O'Boyle, Archbishop of Washington. Signers of the call for the March were:

A. Philip Randolph, President, the Negro-American Labor Council; Roy Wilkins, Executive Secretary of the NAACP; James Farmer, National Director, Congress of Racial Equality; Whitney M. Young, Jr., Executive Director, National Urban League; Dr. Martin Luther King, Jr., President, Southern Christian Leadership Conference; Walter Reuther, President, United Auto Workers; Rabbi Jochim Prinz, President, American Jewish Congress; Matthew Ahmann, Executive Director, National Catholic Conference for Interracial Justice; The Reverend Eugene Carson Blake, Vice-Chairman, National Council of Churches; and John Lewis, Chairman, Student Nonviolent Coordinating Committee. Standing also at left in photo are Dr. Ralph J. Bunche of the United Nations and Bayard Rustin, who read the demands; and at far right, Dr. Benjamin E. Mays, President, Morehouse College, who asked the benediction.

In the spring and summer of 1963, there had been the vicious policemen, their dogs, their firehoses, their cruel faces as they sat on and mercilessly beat Black men, women, and children in the U.S. southland. Via television, the nation watched. And from the narrow confines of his jail cell, Dr. Martin Luther King, Jr., scribbled and passed to a co-worker from the outside his magnificent epistle, "Letter from a Birmingham Jail." The nation—especially the critical white clergy whom he challenged to join rather than criticize the Movement toward justice—read it, many with compassion. These events were catalytic. The time had come. And in early July, with the marshalling of forces by labor leader A. Philip Randolph, there issued from the leaders of major civil rights organizations the call heard around the world: a march on Washington.

The March leaders' statement on the printed program captured, in advance, the mood, purpose, and spirit of the March:

"The Washington March of August 28th is more than just a demonstration.

"It was conceived as an outpouring of the deep feeling of millions of white and colored American citizens that the time has come for the government of the United States of America, and particularly for the Congress of that government, to grant and guarantee complete equality in citizenship to the Negro minority of our population.

"As such, the Washington March is a living petition—in the flesh—of the scores of thousands of citizens of both races who will be present from all parts of our country.

"It will be orderly, but not subservient. It will be proud, but not arrogant. It will be non-violent, but not timid. It will be unified in purposes and behavior, not splintered into groups and individual competitors. It will be outspoken, but not raucous.

"It will have the dignity befitting a demonstration in behalf of the human rights of twenty millions of people, with the eye and the judgment of the world focused upon Washington, D.C., on August 28, 1963.

"In a neighborhood dispute there may be stunts, rough words and even hot insults; but when a whole people speaks to its government, the dialogue and the action must be on a level reflecting the worth of that people and the responsibility of that government.

"We, the undersigned, who see the Washington March as wrapping up the dreams, hopes, ambitions, tears, and prayers of millions who have lived for this day, call upon the members, followers and wellwishers of our several organizations to make the March a disciplined and purposeful demonstration.

"We call upon them all, black and white, to resist provocations to disorder and to violence.

"We ask them to remember that evil persons are determined to smear this March and to discredit the cause of equality by deliberate efforts to stir disorder.

"We call for self-discipline, so that no one in our own ranks, however enthusiastic, shall be the spark for disorder.

"We call for resistance to the efforts of those who, while not enemies of the March as such, might seek to use it to advance causes not dedicated primarily to civil rights or the welfare of our country.

"We ask each and every one in attendance in Washington or in spiritual attendance back home to place the Cause above all else.

"Do not permit a few irresponsible people to hang a new problem around our necks as we return home. Let's do what we came to do—place the national human rights problem squarely on the doorstep of the national Congress and of the Federal Government.

"Let's win at Washington."

Heroine of modern civil rights movement, Mrs. Rosa Parks, *in 1955, refused order to surrender her seat to a white man on back of a bus in Montgomery, Ala. After day's work as a seamstress, Mrs. Parks said she was tired and was insulted by the bus driver's order. Her arrest prompted a call to local NAACP leader, E. D. Nixon, who, in turn, asked the help of a new, 26-year-old preacher, Dr. Martin Luther King, Jr. After boycott succeeded, Mrs. Parks moved to Detroit. This photograph shows Mrs. Parks in Washington, being honored by the Congressional Black Caucus in 1982.*

New protest style for the 1960s and 1970s was set by 1963 march.

JOHN H. JOHNSON (under "No U.S. Dough" sign), highly successful publisher of Ebony *and* Jet *magazines, symbolized support of the Black non-poor as well as poor.*

Style of dress bespoke quiet dignity and substantial level of March support. Upper right, W. Sumter McIntosh, civil rights leader from Dayton, Ohio, reached to greet a friend, was later shot fatally while trying to prevent a crime on Dayton street. Lower right, Sammy Davis, Jr., actor Robert Ryan and other entertainers and artists were prominent in crowd.

Actor Burt Lancaster (upper left) dramatically unravels scroll with thousands of signatures from Europe in support of March. (Lower left), Although not a major issue on March agenda, war was a concern of some. Later, Dr. King strongly embraced peace as integral to issue of justice. (Upper right) Peter, Paul & Mary entertained at 1963 March and again in 1983. (Lower right) Unprecedented in its size, the 1963 March was also unprecedented in its bringing together such diverse backgrounds of race, religion, culture, and economics.

Congressman Adam Clayton Powell, *Democrat from Harlem, drew great applause when he "delivered" a massive congressional delegation to the steps of Lincoln Memorial. It assuaged the fears of many that the marchers would suffer violence, either from the police or by others not halted by the police. One of only four Black members of Congress in 1963, Powell chaired the House Education and Labor Committee and fostered President Lyndon B. Johnson's Great Society programs, including the federal anti-poverty program.*

3 Threats to the Dream

Dr. King's dream that character—not color—would be the grounds for judging people was also a dream that Klanism and Klan violence would cease. Neither did. Indeed, the Ku Klux Klan boasted a resurgence in the early 1980s.

When Dr. King dreamed of the races being able to "work together," he dreamed, of course, that there would be jobs—for people as well as for computers. Between the marches, however, computers, robotics and related technology displaced human workers by the hundreds of thousands. One result was the highest unemployment since the Great Depression of the 1930s.

And his dream of transforming "the jangling discords of our nation into a beautiful symphony of brotherhood" was set by his comrades' efforts to promote peace and justice abroad, as well as at home. Longtime Jewish allies objected to the insertion of "Peace" into the 1983 march theme—"Jobs, Peace, and Freedom." To them, "Peace" somehow threatened the security of Israel.

These were among the major threats to Dr. King's 1963 dream when some 500,000 proclaimed "We Still Have a Dream" at the 20th Anniversary March in 1983.

Two days before the march, members of a three-year-old Anti-Klan Network set up an information vigil and press conference in front of the Justice Department in Washington. They complained that, once again, innocent Black, Jewish, and other citizens were being shot, beaten, and subjected to other forms of abuse by the Klan.

In some cases—as in the case of five social activists fatally gunned down in Greensboro, N.C., in 1979—the Klansmen guilty of the crimes go free. The Anti-Klan group charged that the Justice Department did not vigorously investigate, prevent, or prosecute Klan violence.

Indeed, the Klan resurgence included public demonstrations in such unlikely places as suburban Montgomery County, Maryland, and in the Nation's Capital itself. In each of those demonstrations, however, massive crowd opposition forced police protection of the Klan members. However narrowly, in the end, the First Amendment rights of the Klan were upheld.

Even if the Klan's rights were not in jeopardy, other aspects of Dr. King's dream were.

As Voltaire realized, "Work helps preserve us from three great evils—weariness, vice, and want." Dr. King preached against those evils, as well. But all three rose visibly between 1963 and 1983, as the loss of jobs to automation and policies of government also rose sharply.

Job loss was most severe among Black men and Black youths.

Between 1974 and 1975, for example, while white unemployment doubled from 4.2 percent to 8.8 percent, Black unemployment rose from 9.5 percent to 15.8 percent. But, while white unemployment at the time of the 1983 march stood at 8.2 percent, Black unemployment had leaped to 20 percent.

Even worse, at the time of the 1983 march, white teenagers were unemployed at a rate of 19.8 percent, and Black teenagers were unemployed at a rate of 53 percent—more than one out of two.

As Voltaire might have warned, such lack of work was accompanied by rises in crime and poverty, but also in weariness and desperation indicated by drug abuse, which became so epidemic as to give rise to the description—"chemical people."

Exactly one year before his death by assassination on April 4, 1968, Dr. King spoke out against the war in Vietnam, and accused the U.S. military-industrialists of being the world's worst "purveyors of violence."

Faithful to Dr. King's search for peace and justice through non-violence, a delegation of 10 persons from the Southern Christian Leadership Conference journeyed to Lebanon in 1979 in an effort to persuade Arabs and Israelis to renounce violence.

Led by SCLC President Joseph E. Lowery and Congressman Walter E. Fauntroy, chairman of the SCLC Board, the delegates met with many Arab and Christian factions in Lebanon, and, finally with Yasser Arafat, chairman of the Organization for the Liberation of Palestine (PLO).

The Israeli government, however, would not receive the delegation into Israel.

At the end of a dramatic four-hour meeting, Chairman Arafat agreed to ask his council to consider the unilateral non-violence stance proposed by the SCLC. He also joined in a spirited singing of "We Shall Overcome," the anthem of the civil rights movement in the United States.

In 1982, Israel invaded Lebanon, causing wide-spread loss of life and destruction. Chairman Arafat, and those comrades who survived with him, were forced by the Israeli Army to leave Lebanon.

The Israeli Army remained in Lebanon.

Shortly after the PLO military forces had left, however, the world was shocked by the massacre of some 3,000 helpless men, women, and children in two Palestinian refugee camps guarded by the Israeli Army.

These events, given the SCLC peace efforts in Lebanon and its leadership in the 1983 march, splintered the historic alliance between the civil rights movement and many Jewish organizations.

STOP THE KKK!

Washington, D.C., November 27

Be where the Klan says they're going to start their march!

Rally 10 a.m. Saturday — First St. N.W. & Constitution Ave.

In D.C. Now and Everywhere, Fight Klan Terror!

For Labor/Black Mobilization Against Racist Terror!

These Klansmen paraded in the restricted area of a public park in Montgomery County, Md., in 1982, heavily guarded by police. Several months later, the Klan sought to parade in the Nation's Capital, but were met with massive counter-demonstrations bearing anti-Klan slogans (upper right).

A Traditional Threat:
Resurgence of the Ku Klux Klan

In the shadow of the Capitol, in downtown Washington, and in prosperous Montgomery County, Md., the police (including a Black woman) protected Klan from counter-demonstrators in 1982-83.

Veteran civil rights workers Mrs. Anne Braden and the Rev. Mac Charles Jones embrace as Anti-Klan Network official recites Klan atrocities to Washington new media.

Mrs. Julia Chaney Moss and Mrs. Carolyn Goodman, sister and mother of civil rights workers killed in Mississippi in 1964, said massive public pressure is necessary to stop the Klan.

In front of anti-Klan display outside Justice Department, John McCollum identified himself photographed after Klan shot and nearly blinded him to "teach him a lesson" in Alabama in 1978. No one went to trial, McCollum said.

THE RIGHT OF THE PEOPLE
TO KEEP AND BEAR ARMS
SHALL NOT BE INFRINGED

A Non-Traditional Threat:
Technology and the Displacement of Man

Robot, in the Japan Pavilion, 1982 World's Fair, Knoxville, Tenn. (Right) Occupationally displaced persons, Washington, D.C.

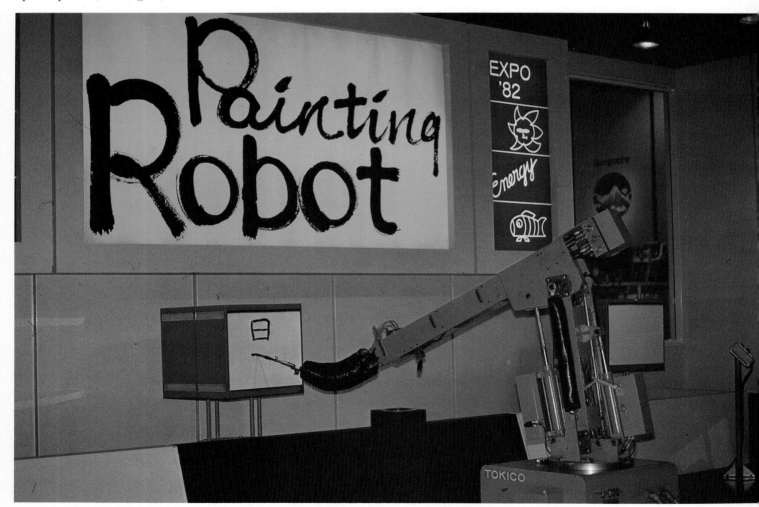

"Society everywhere is in conspiracy against the manhood of every one of its members."
—Ralph Waldo Emerson

"Work helps preserve us from three great evils—weariness, vice, and want."

    —Voltaire

"Work, or lose the power to will, lose the power to love."

    —John Sullivan Dwight

A New Threat:
The Unacceptability of Peace

For generations, American Jews had been the most immediate and reliable ally in civil rights. Black people, themselves, felt a kinship to whatever problems of religious and racial bigotry were also suffered by Jews. Unsurprisingly, then, the American Jewish Congress was quick to join Black leaders in their call for a "March on Washington for Jobs and Freedom" in 1963. Jews and Black Americans were allies.

But, when the call went out for a 1983 "March on Washington for Jobs, Peace, and Freedom," the American Jewish Congress said no. So did other Jewish organizations, including the Jewish War Veterans, B'nai B'rith, the Jewish Defense League, and the American Jewish Committee.

The difference was "peace."

It was not merely the insertion of "peace" into the 1983 March theme. It was also the pursuit of peace in far-away Lebanon by a delegation of the Southern Christian Leadership Conference.

Many Jews read the "peace" theme as a call for cuts in the billions of dollars in military and other aid the U.S. annually sends to the State of Israel. They also wished punishment on two of the 1983 March leaders: Dr. Joseph E. Lowery, third president of the Southern Christian Leadership Conference, founded by Dr. King; and Congressman Walter E. Fauntroy, SCLC Board chairman and director of the 1983 March.

In 1979, the two men had committed what was, to many Jews, the unpardonable crime of sitting down in Beirut and discussing peace with Yasser Arafat, chairman of the Organization for the Liberation of Palestine.

A short time earlier, the U.S. Ambassador to the United Nations, Andrew Young, had met briefly in New York with the PLO's UN observer, Zhadi Labib Terzi. News reports of their having met were followed by Jewish complaints to President Carter, which were followed by Ambassador Young's sudden resignation.

Two weeks before the 1983 March, the American Jewish Congress recanted, and pledged support—but only after March leaders agreed to policy language that did not specifically call for cuts in U.S. military aid to Israel. Ultimately, the American Jewish Congregation and B'nai B'rith also joined the 1983 march.

In the spring of 1982, Israel invaded Lebanon, resulting in the loss of thousands of lives, many of them innocent civilians. Particularly tragic and bestial were the massacres of some 3,000 Palestine men, women, and children in two West Beirut refugee camps—Sabra and Shatila—guarded by the Isaeli Army.

On October 11, 1979, a few weeks after the 10-member SCLC delegation returned from Lebanon, Congressman Fauntroy reported to his House colleagues on his "fact-finding mission." Below, and on the ensuing pages, lines from his one-hour presentation are used to help tell the story of what he saw, and why an aversion to peace is a major threat to The Dream.

"The Palestinians fear that Israel's intention is to exterminate those Palestinians who steadfastly hold to the goal of self-determination and a Palestinian homeland. That fear gives rise to acts of violence in what Palestinians call 'occupied Palestine' designed to remind Israelis that there will be no peace until there is justice and a homeland for the Palestinians. That violence generates a hatred among the Israelis that feeds their cycle of fear, violence and hatred even as their violence feeds the same cycle among the Palestinians.

"The Phalangist Christians fear being engulfed by a sea of Moslems. That fear feeds the violence and counter violence that generates an intense hatred among and between the PLO and the Phalangists.

"Lebanese Government officials fear that it is the Israeli intention to balkanize Lebanon and, indeed, the entire Middle East into warring camps among Christians and Moselms to assure Israeli military dominance of the region. The violence visited upon Lebanese villages, Lebanese citizens and Palestinians in Lebanon by the Israelis, a violence which the Lebanese Government has no capacity to return, gives rise to an intense hatred among Lebanese of what they call the 'racist, Zionist expansionists' in Israel."

"Observe good faith and justice toward all nations. Cultivate peace and harmony with all. . . . The Nation which indulges toward another an habitual hatred or an habitual fondness is in some degree a slave. It is a slave to its animosity or to its affection, either of which is sufficient to lead it astray from its duty and its interest."

—George Washington
Farewell Address (1794)

"We went to express our heartfelt and overriding concern for the human suffering and misery of our brothers and sisters on all sides of the Middle East conflict who are caught up in the injustice which comes from a reliance upon violent strategies for change."

"In addition to this moral commitment to the efficacy of peace through nonviolence, we went to Lebanon armed with the essential facts which told us of the cycle of violence and counterviolence between the PLO and Israel, and other combatants in the region."

"Injustice anywhere is a threat to justice everywhere."

—Martin Luther King, Jr.
Letter from the Birmingham Jail
(1963)

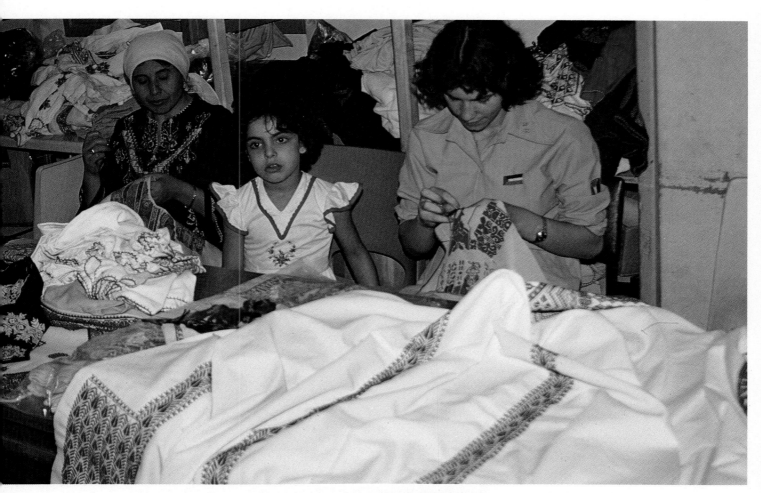

"We knew of the long history of events which had pushed Palestinians out of that land and made them refugees all over the Middle East, and of the struggle of our Jewish brothers to create a homeland, particularly after the atrocities of Hitler in Nazi Germany and throughout Europe."

"While in Lebanon, we met with the President, Premier, foreign minister, and deputy Speaker of the House of the Government of Lebanon, and parties on virtually all sides of the dispute, including the PLO, the Christian Phalangist Party, the Lebanese Islamic Council, the Lebanese National Movement, and the Middle East Council of Churches. We came away with a picture of human beings, all of whom are our brothers under the skin, caught up in a vicious cycle of fear, violence, and hate which only a compassionate, understanding, and reasonably detached world community can assist them in breaking."

"We saw for ourselves the balkanization of the city of Beirut and areas of the country out of a distrust which establishes geographical checkpoints controlled by the Palestinians, the Christian Militia, the Syrians, the Lebanese National Army and the United Nations. We witnessed the violation of the sovereign air space of Lebanon by Israeli aircraft with the distrustful objective of carrying out surveillance over the whole of the country."

"Further, I will say that regardless of the response to our proposals from the PLO, our Government should continue to attempt to develop a legitimate, open, and substantive dialogue with the PLO. It was our experience that far from being the 'bloodthirsty killer' and 'wild-eyed terrorist' the Western press has made of him, Mr. Arafat appears reasonable and open to dialogue within the framework of the interest of his own people."

"To our outrage, we saw unmistakable evidence of the use of American weapons on nonmilitary targets. I have returned with shrapnel, parts of exploded shells and cluster bombs which I lifted from the ruins of bombed-out Palestinian and Lebanese villages in Lebanon."

"On the other hand, we have been seriously concerned about the Israeli Government's attitude toward all peace initiatives as reflected in its rejection of our request for a hearing on the peace proposals."

"And last, but not least, we were successful in illustrating by our mission, that we take seriously the material costs to us as black Americans in any area of the world where the United States has a vital stake and that we will not be silenced or excluded from participation in those decisions which affect our lives and the well-being of this country.

"The initiatives taken by Dr. Joseph E. Lowery, and me, to achieve peace through nonviolence in the Middle East, have become the source of great controversy here in the United States. This, of course, is not the first time that we, in the S.C.L.C., have run into controversy over the assertion of our right to speak out on questions of our Nation's foreign policy. On April 4, 1967, our president, Dr. Martin Luther King, Jr., took a stand on the Vietnam war. He said the time had come for us to abandon violent strategies for achieving peace in Southeast Asia.

"Dr. Martin Luther King then and the Southern Christian Leadership Conference now takes its stand for peace through nonviolence, not because it is safe or popular or politic, but because conscience tells us that it is right."

4 1983: They Still Have a Dream

God forbid we should ever be 20 years without such a rebellion. The people cannot be all, and always, well informed. . . . If they remain quiet . . . it is a lethargy, a forerunner of death to the public liberty.
   —*Thomas Jefferson*

Power concedes nothing without a demand. It never did, and it never will. Find out just what people will submit to, and you have found out the exact amount of injustice and wrong which will be imposed upon them.
   —*Frederick Douglass*

With this faith, we will be able to work together, to pray together, to struggle together, to go to jail together, to stand up for freedom together, knowing that we will be free one day.
   —*Martin Luther King, Jr.*

August 28, 1963, was a one-time thing. A cosmic moment it seemed, when the quarter-million souls gathered at the Lincoln Memorial, and the untold millions they represented before and after them, were configured in such a way that heaven and earth would hear an unforgettable message—distilled from the genius of a people long and bitterly oppressed. It was, as Dr. Martin Luther King, Jr. said, the message of a dream "deeply rooted in the American dream." It was, no doubt, also deeply rooted in an African understanding of life's continuum embracing the dead, the living, and the unborn; they all seemed to come together in the life and dream of Dr. King.

Unsurprisingly, then, the spirit and courage of Dr. King were invoked 20 years later, when conditions of struggle and opportunity needed his presence. Mrs. Coretta Scott King, Dr. King's widow and director of the Martin Luther King Center for Non-Violent Social Change in Atlanta, Congressman Walter E. Fauntroy, Washington director of the 1963 march, and others seized the opportunity.

In their "Call to the Nation," they addressed the conditions:

Three critical conditions in our society—insufferable unemployment; an escalating arms race; and the denial of basic rights and programs which ensure freedom— force the undersigned to call upon our fellow Americans to March on Washington on August 28, 1983 on the occasion of the Twentieth Anniversary of the historic March on Washington.

Thus, the "20th Anniversary March for Jobs, Peace, and Freedom," bringing together a "Coalition of Conscience."

Washington's Metro transit fare of flat 50¢ per ride for the day helped move crowds, such as these arriving by subway.

Young marcher begins day fortified with orange juice.

Especially welcome were children of Dr. King and his SCLC successor, Dr. Ralph D. Abernathy. L to R: Yolanda, Bernice, Martin III, Ralph Abernathy, Jr., and Dexter.

Mass of students marched five miles from Howard to Monument grounds, shouting such as, "We're all fired up, ain't gonna take it anymore!"

"*If a man does not keep pace with his companions, perhaps it is because he hears a different drummer. Let him step to the music which he hears, however measured or far away.*"
—*Henry David Thoreau*

Diversity of "the Rainbow Coalition" included children, seniors, young professionals, retirees, gays and lesbians, politicians, racial, religious, ethnic, and national groups, all proclaiming a common ethic of brotherhood and peace espoused by Dr. King.

Colors of the "Rainbow"

"'A fair day's wage for a fair day's work': it is as just a demand as governed men ever made of governing. It is the everlasting right of man."
—Thomas Carlyle

Various factions emphasized one aspect of the march slogan, "Jobs, Peace, and Freedom." For some, it was jobs.

For others, the emphasis was peace, or at least, the absence of nuclear war.

This group demanded freedom from threat of
genocide, under banners of Black nationalist
leaders Malcolm X and Marcus Garvey.

"More than an end to war, we want an end to the beginnings of all wars."
—Franklin D. Roosevelt (1945)

Indian and Hispanic groups demanded freedom from poor education and from oppression
in Central America.

*rab-Americans, not a factor in the 1963 march,
~gured prominently in 1983 march as march
~aders continued year-long effort to bring non-
~olent resolution to Arab-Israeli settlement of
~alestinian issue.*

*American Indians brought their plight to rally's
attention.*

Assembly point—the Mall stretching eastward from the Washington Monument to the U.S. Capitol—began to fill at about 8 a.m. The yellow-topped bandstand—seen here from atop the Washington Monument—featured an inspirational program of speakers and entertainers for nearly three hours, until March leaders stepped off for Lincoln Memorial shortly before noon.

By noon, marchers from Mall area were pouring into the main rally site at Lincoln Memorial, alongside Reflecting Pool.

Massive crowds of marchers mixed in with leaders, preventing smooth step-off, and moved enthusiastically from Mall northward to Constitution Avenue.

At intersection of 17th and Constitution, police line protects march route as bands and banners lend festive air to petitioning of government.

Marchers, still pouring into Lincoln Memorial grounds, hear call for invocation. Great hush fills historic site, as marchers bow heads for prayer opening the rally.

March program formally opens with invocation offered by Washington Archbishop James A. Hickey. His predecessor, Archbishop Patrick O'Boyle, offered invocation at 1963 march.

Pete Seeger

Sammy Davis

Bill Cosby and wi[

Gloria Steinem

Billy Davis and Marilyn McCoo

Peter, Paul and Mary

Odetta

Dick Gregory

Ossie Davis, actor, addressed assembly rallies in 1963 and 1983.

Dr. Ralph David Abernathy, founding vice-president, Southern Christian Leadership Conference (SCLC), immediate successor to Dr. King as president.

Congressman Peter Rodino (D-N.J.), chairman, House Judiciary Committee, presided over impeachment hearings of Richard M. Nixon, attended rally in 1963 also.

Former Vice President Walter F. Mondale, a favorite of labor and educational groups, feared that Jesse Jackson candidacy might draw off Mondale support in 1984 presidential campaign.

Reunion of civil rights battlers the Rev. Fred Shuttlesworth, who suffered violence in Birmingham in 1960s, and the Rev. C. T. Vivian, chairman, National Anti-Klan Network.

Seeking relief from intense heat, Congressman Parren J. Mitchell (D-Md.) dons handkerchief. Member of strong civil rights family in Baltimore, Mitchell is chairman of the House Committee on Small Business, former chairman of the Congressional Black Caucus.

Congressmen John Conyers, Jr. (D-Mich.) and Ronald Dellums (D-Calif.) helped increase number of Black congressmen from four to 21 between 1963 and 1983. A member of the House Judiciary Committee, Conyers sponsored bill that made Martin Luther King, Jr.'s birthday a national holiday. Dellums chairs House District Committee.

...rthur S. Flemming, secretary of Health, Education and Welfare during Eisenhower Administration, later served as chairman of U.S. ...ommission on Civil Rights.

77

Also exercising a First Amendment right—a free press—an international press corps gave extensive coverage, including some live radio and TV broadcasts, in contrast to sparse coverage given the 1963 March.

Joseph L. Rauh, longtime Washington civil liberties lawyer, among early arrivers.

Civil rights husband-and-wife team: lawyers Juanita Jackson Mitchell and the late Clarence Mitchell, Jr. Members of Baltimore families prominent in fights for racial justice, she argued civil rights cases in the Brown era, he was chief NAACP Washington lobbyist for 30 years.

Roy Ennis, national director of Congress of Racial Equality (CORE), played no official role in 1983 March, although his predecessor, James Farmer, was a convener of the 1963 March.

...rnon Jordan (center, wearing tie) sits quietly in ...served area behind podium. In 1982, Jordan ...signed as head of National Urban League, ...hich was a convener of 1963 March but did not ...ficially participate in 1983 March.

Congressman Charles B. Rangel (D-N.Y.), succeeded the late popular Harlem Congressman Adam Clayton Powell, who escorted scores of congressmen to 1963 March.

Clyde Bellecourt, of the American Indian Movement (AIM), reminded the crowd of crimes of early settlers against native Americans. A convener of the 1983 March, he said crimes against his people continue.

At the Podium. . .

ational Director of the 20th Anniversary
arch, and Washington Director for 1963
arch, Congressman Walter E. Fauntroy opens
083 March.

ella Abzug, of Women USA, is a former Member
Congress from New York, and a convener of
083 March.

Atlanta Mayor Andrew Young, a convener of
1983 March, was voter education director in
early days of SCLC, and close aide to Dr. King. He
left Congress to serve a tumultuous, abbreviated
tenure as President Carter's Ambassador to
United Nations.

Rabbi Alex Schindler, of the Union of American Hebrew Congregations, unlike some other Jewish leaders, was an early and continuing supporter of 1983 March.

Former Senator James Abourezk, head of American Arab Discrimination Committee, and convener of 1983 March, reminded marchers that Israeli denial of Palestinian homeland was at heart of Middle-East strife.

Literary great Maya Angelou was one of several emcees.

Mrs. Myrlie Evers (right) is widow of Mississippi NAACP leader Medgar Evers, whose unpunished assassination in 1963 sparked demands for legal justice at 1963 March.

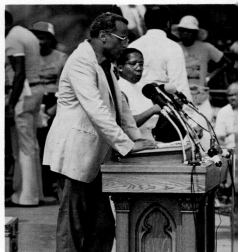

Singer Harry Belafonte supported civil rights with benefit concerts during 1960s, was convener of 1983 March.

Known as "Daddy King" to generations, Martin Luther King, Sr., proudly addresses 20th Anniversary crowd on the arms of three grandchildren.

Dr. Joseph Lowery, president of the Southern Christian Leadership Conference, chairs National Black Leadership Forum of 16 groups, and was convener of 1983 March.

Poet Audre Lorde, gay/lesbian speaker.

Minister Louis Farrakhan (center), of the Nation of Islam, listens with interest to dozens of speeches before his turn at podium. A late addition to speaking program, his organization did not participate in 1963 March.

Judy Goldsmith, president of the National Organization for Women (NOW), urged political action for and by women. She was a convener of 1983 March.

Jesse Jackson's address drew chants of "Run, Jesse, Run." Julian Bond, Georgia State Senator, got nomination speech for vice-president in 1972.

Musical genius Stevie Wonder, ardent supporter of holiday in honor of Dr. Martin Luther King, Jr., wrote and sang a song in support, crowd enthusiastically chants its support.

"This is your day, Martin," widow Mrs. Coretta Scott King said. Audience was visibly moved at hearing recording of Dr. King's famous "I Have a Dream" speech from the 1963 March. Standing with Mrs. King are their children Dexter, Yolanda, Bernice, and Martin III.

NAACP executive director Benjamin Hooks discussed significance of the march with student reporters Orlando Ledbetter and Henry B. Hall of Howard University. Donna Brazille, coordinator of March, receives congratulations at day's end, then became director of new lobbying office for "Coalition of Conscience." Diversity of marchers is shown by clown, still smiling at day's end, and several of the scores of handicapped persons also active in the March.

Peaceable assembly of 1983 march, like its 1963 predecessor, ended at dusk, leaving demonstrators to pursue rights back home, and leaving the Mall calm, still nobly inviting.

I learned that the essential character of a nation is determined not by the upper classes, but by the common people, and that the common people of all nations are truly brothers in the great family of mankind. . . . Even as I grew to feel more Negro in spirit, or African as I put it then, I also came to feel a sense of oneness with the white working people whom I came to know and love.

This belief in the oneness of humankind . . . has existed within me side by side with my deep attachment to the cause of my own race.
—Paul Robeson

They cooped you in their kitchens,
The penned you in their factories,
They gave you the jobs that they were too good for,
They tried to guarantee happiness to themselves
By shunting dirt and misery to you . . .

One thing they cannot prohibit—
  The strong men . . . coming on
  The strong men gittin' stronger.
  Strong men . . .
  Stronger . . .
    —Sterling A. Brown
    (From "Strong Men")

" **And finally, even as we struggle for survival and for our own self-fulfillment, we must struggle for a coalition with and for a time of clarity for the white masses in this country, a struggle with them for their ultimate understanding that what is good for Black people is good for the entire masses of this nation.**"

—John Oliver Killens (1982)
Foreword to the republication of *The Choice*, by Samuel F. Yette.

On November 3, 10 weeks after the 1983 march, the Rev. Jesse L. Jackson, at 43, former SCLC executive, and founder of Operation PUSH, declared, as a Democrat, his presidential candidacy at Washington Convention Center.

5 Some Fulfillments

In the spring of 1968, barely a month before the assassination of Dr. Martin Luther King, Jr., the National Advisory Commission on Civil Disorders issued its report. Commonly known as the Riot Commission, appointed by President Lyndon B. Johnson, it deeply implicated "white society" in the nation's epidemic of violence, and otherwise stunned the nation with its report:

This is our basic conclusion: Our nation is moving toward two societies, one black, one white—separate and unequal.

Fifteen years later, a few months before the historic 1983 march for "Jobs, Peace, and Freedom," the Washington-based Joint Center for Political Studies issued "A Policy Framework for Racial Justice." Culminated by a group of Black scholars and the Black Leadership Forum, the Framework offered a striking and progressively disturbing conclusion:

At least three societies exist in America today: The mainstream, the assimilated minorities, and the excluded. These three societies are separate and unequal and the disparities among them threaten to destroy the national fabric.

Each conclusion spoke to moods and conditions prevailing in the period of the respective marches—the two-decade period of the early 1960s and 1980s. And, although the splintering had seemed to grow from two to three segments, another development of tremendous significance and potential was also underway: From the threatened "national fabric," the drive of Black Americans for justice and survival had begun to discover and weave common threads between and within the three societies—mainstream, achieving minorities, and the excluded of various races and classes.

Thus, another striking conclusion seems available and compelling: Although enemies of survival and justice are still massively arrayed against the nation's historically oppressed, between 1963 and 1983 there *was* movement by members of oppressed groups into unprecedented areas of power, recognition, and power potential.

And thus, Dr. King's dream of transforming injustice and "jangling discords," while far from realized, did advance along the lines of coalition and clarity envisioned by the distinguished writer and humanist, John Oliver Killens.

Some success in the Black American's struggle for coalition and clarity with others has resulted in the beginnings of a truly historic and providential development—the transformation of *Black leadership* into *national leadership*.

Such transformation—a culmination of the Third American Revolution—has two bases in ancient and modern American history:

1 Ancient injustices as deep as slavery and "manifest destiny," and modern injustices as current as undeclared war against the survival the Palestinian people, who stand in the way of a new "manifest destiny."

2 The pragmatism of white Americans, who, with whatever public reluctance, privately realize that the potential for nuclear destruction and other human sufferings is greater at the hands of traditional white leadership, and that Afro-Americans, whom they know and trust, have for centuries endured the injustice and insanity of others, and have emerged able, loving, and willing to serve the best interests of all.

Thus, the move by the successors of Dr. King to perceive and include peace as a major issue—indeed, as a right of all people—is a move of great catalytic potential.

The issue of jobs, a constant demand by Black civil rights groups for decades, is no longer the near-exclusive demand of Black workers. Technology, and further advancements by power-elite capitalists have forced non-elite whites to see their own self-interests best protected by the worker rights of Black heroes for justice.

Technology, undeclared wars, and other threats to the proper functioning of the Constitution have radically eroded the constitutionally-protected rights for virtually everyone. As basic rights are visibly eroded, the historically Black demand for "freedom" gains new meaning for the nation's masses, in general.

Thus, while the two and three-society divisions occur at one level, the receptivity of protest, the drum-majoring for justice, widened broadly in the 1963-83 period. That wider appeal is a form of progress, even power.

In 1983, more than in any previous year, the effects of the wider appeal of Black protest became evident. The best publicized and most significant events were each unprecedented forms of power:

1 Vanessa Williams, of New York, was crowned "Miss America."

2 Colonel Guion Bluford entered space as the first Black U.S. astronaut.

3 Congress passed, and President Ronald Reagan signed a bill making January 15, the birthday of Dr. Martin Luther King, Jr., a national holiday.

4 The Rev. Jesse Jackson, with high visibility and wide coalition support, announced his candidacy for the Democratic presidential nomination, the first Black candidate given a "serious" chance to affect the presidential outcome.

Vanessa Williams, "Miss America," symbolized Black transformation to national recognition, broke pageant's 63-year-old color barrier. Her runner-up (right), Suzette Charles, was "Miss New Jersey".

National Conference of Black Mayors president Johnny Ford, of Tuskegee, Ala., presents Vanessa Williams, "Miss America 1984," and members of her court at Washington reception. Accompanying "Miss America" are Suzette Charles ("Miss New Jersey," 1st Runner-up), and, at right, Amy Keys ("Miss Maryland").

Astronaut Guion Bluford, in exchange of gifts, presented to Washington Mayor Marion Barry collage of take-off that made Colonel Bluford first Black U.S. astronaut.

Before signing Martin Luther King, Jr. Holiday Bill, President Reagan praised Dr. King's contribution to the nation. After the signing, Mrs. King expressed thanks for the nation's "highest recognition" for her late husband. With them on the dais (l. to. r.) are: Mrs. Christine Farris, Dr. King's sister; Vice-President George Bush; Arthur Fletcher, former assistant Secretary of Labor; Congressman Robert Garcia (D-N.Y.); Clarence Thomas, Chairman, Equal Employment Opportunity Commission; Senate Majority Leader Howard Baker, Jr. (R-Tenn.); Senator Joseph R. Biden, Jr. (R-Del.); Senator Charles McC. Mathias, Jr. (R-Md.); Senator Edward M. Kennedy (D-Mass.); Senator Robert Dole (R-Kans.); Congressman Jack F. Kemp, (R-N.Y.); Congresswoman Katie Hall (D-Ind.), sponsor of King Holiday Bill; Samuel Pierce, Jr., Secretary, Housing and Urban Development; Stephen Rhodes, Advisor to the Vice-President; and Melvin Bradley, Advisor to the President.

Holiday Honoring Martin Luther King, Jr.

President Reagan

. . . Martin Luther King was born in 1929 in an America where, because of the color of their skin, nearly 1 in 10 lived lives that were separate and unequal. Most black Americans were taught in segregated schools. Across the country, too many could find only poor jobs, toiling for low wages. They were refused entry into hotels and restaurants, made to use separate facilities. In a nation that proclaimed liberty and justice for all, too many black Americans were living with neither.

In one city, a rule required all blacks to sit in the rear of public buses. But in 1955, when a brave woman named Rosa Parks was told to move to the back of the bus, she said, "No." A young minister in a local Baptist church, Martin Luther King, then organized a boycott of the bus company—a boycott that stunned the country. Within 6 months the courts had ruled the segregation of public transportation unconstitutional.

Dr. King had awakened something strong and true, a sense that true justice must be colorblind, and that among white and black Americans, as he put it, "Their destiny is tied up with our destiny, and their freedom is inextricably bound to our freedom; we cannot walk alone."

. . . Dr. King's work brought him to this city often. And in one sweltering August day in 1963, he addressed a quarter of a million people at the Lincoln Memorial. If American history grows from two centuries to twenty, his words that day will never be forgotten. "I have a dream that one day on the red hills of Georgia, the sons of former slaves and the sons of former slave owners will be able to sit down together at the table of brotherhood."

In 1968 Martin Luther King was gunned down by a brutal assassin, his life cut short at the age of 39. But those 39 short years had changed America forever. The Civil Rights Act of 1964 had guaranteed all Americans equal use of public accommodations, equal access to programs fi-

nanced by Federal funds, and the right to compete for employment on the sole basis of individual merit. The Voting Rights Act of 1965 had made certain that from then on black Americans would get to vote. But most important, there was no just a change of law; there was a change of heart. The conscience of America had been touched. Across the land, people had begun to treat each other not as blacks and whites, but as fellow Americans.

. . . Now our nation has decided to honor Dr. Martin Luther King, Jr., by setting aside a day each year to remember him and the just cause he stood for. We've made historic strides since Rosa Parks refused to go to the back of the bus. As a democratic people, we can take pride in the knowledge that we Americans recognized a grave injustice and took action to correct it. And we should remember that in far too many countries, people like Dr. King never have the opportunity to speak out at all.

Mrs. King

Thank you, Mr. President, Vice President Bush, Majority Leader Baker and the distinguished Congressional and Senatorial delegations, and other representatives who've gathered here, and friends.

All right-thinking people, all right-thinking Americans are joined in spirit with us this day as the highest recognition which this nation gives is bestowed upon Martin Luther King, Jr., one who also was the recipient of the highest recognition which the world bestows, the Nobel Peace Prize.

In his own life's example, he symbolized what was right about America, what was noblest and best, what human beings have pursued since the beginning of history. He loved unconditionally. He was in constant pursuit of truth, and when he discovered it, he embraced it. His non-violent campaigns brought redemption, reconciliation, and justice. He taught us that only peaceful means can bring about peaceful ends, that our goal was to create the love community.

America is a more democratic nation, a more just nation, a more peaceful nation because Martin Luther King, Jr., became her preeminent nonviolent commander.

Martin Luther King, Jr., and his spirit live within all of us. Thank God for the blessing of his life and his leadership and his commitment. What manner of man was this? May we make ourselves worthy to carry on his dream and create the love community.

Thank you.

But traces of bigotry still mar America. So, each year on Martin Luther King Day, let us not only recall Dr. King, but rededicate ourselves to the commandments he believed in and sought to live every day: Thou shall love thy God with all thy heart, and thou shall love thy neighbor as thyself. And I just have to believe that all of us—if all of us, young and old, Republicans and Democrats, do all we can to live up to those commandments, then we will see the day when Dr. King's dream comes true, and in his words, "All of God's children will be able to sing with new meaning, '. . . land where my fathers died, land of the pilgrim's pride, from every mountainside, let freedom ring.'"

Thank you, God bless you, and I will sign it.

On Capitol steps, King family and other supporters of King Holiday Bill celebrated after the bill was signed at the White House. Mrs. King thanked supporters, flanked by nephew Isaac Farris, Jr.;

Dr. King's sister, Mrs. Christine Farris; son, Dexter; son, Martin, III, and SCLC Chairman, Congressman Walter Fauntroy.

"We hold these Truths to be self-evident, that all Men are created equal, that they are endowed by their Creator with certain unalienable Rights, that among these are Life, Liberty, and the Pursuit of Happiness—That to secure these Rights, Governments are instituted among Men, deriving their just Powers from the Consent of the Governed, that whenever any Form of Government becomes destructive of these Ends, it is the Right of the People to alter or to abolish it, and to institute new Government, laying its Foundations on such Principles, and organizing its Powers in such Form, as to them shall seem most likely to effect their Safety and Happiness."

—From the Declaration
of Independence of the
United States of America.